D1390183

OK
To

The Old Testan

MOST OF THE EVENTS OF THE
Testament take place in a small area
the Mediterranean Sea. From ancier
people have lived and travelled alon
land known as the "fertile crescent"
stretches from Egypt, through Cana
Mesopotamia to Babylonia.
There was enough water in this
area to enable them to grow
crops and graze animals.
Canaan, the "promised land",
where the Israelites flourished, is
only about 240km (150 miles)
from north to south. It contains
many different types of scenery,
including plains and river
valleys suitable for farming,
lakes, hills and rocky desert.

Rameses

Moses in
the Bulrushes
GOSHEN
Succoth
Bitte
Lake
Burning Bu

EGYPT

Index

Afrika Corps 13, 16, 19
apartheid 40
atom bomb 26, 29

Baden Powell, Robert 14
Baird, John L. 30
Battle of Britain 10
Belsen 25
Berlin 24, 27, 35, 36, 37, 40
Bevan, Aneurin 38
Bismarck 12
blitz 11, 14
Burma 26, 38

Canada 41
Chamberlain, Neville 8
Chaplin, Charles 11
Chiang Kai-shek 27, 39, 40
China 27, 29, 39, 40
Churchill, Winston 8, 10, 14, 19,
    25, 27, 43
Cold War 31
Cologne 17

D Day 21
De Gaulle, Charles 10, 23, 43
Denmark 8
Disney, Walt 14
Dunkirk 9

Eisenhower, Dwight D. 21, 24, 42
El Alamein 14, 16
Elizabeth, Princess 33, 38

Ford, Henry 34
France 8, 9, 10, 17, 21, 22, 29, 43
Franco, Francisco 34

Gandhi, Mahatma 29, 35
Goering, Hermann 28
Germany 8, 9, 10, 11, 12, 14, 15,
    16, 17, 18, 19, 21, 22, 23, 24, 25,
    27, 28, 29, 35, 36, 37, 43

Hindus 30, 32, 34, 35
Hiroshima 26
Hitler, Adolf 10, 11, 12, 23, 24
Holland (Netherlands) 8
Hong Kong 23

Iron Curtain 29
Israel 35, 36, 37, 39
Italy 13, 18, 19, 22

Japan 13, 16, 23, 24, 26
Johnson, Amy 14

Kon Tiki 34
Kursk 18

Labour Party 27
Lascaux 9
Leyte Gulf 23
Luftwaffe 8, 10, 15

Mao Tse-tung 39, 40
Marshall Plan 32, 33

Mexico 10, 20
Moscow 12
Montgomery, Bernard 16, 43
Moslems 30, 32, 34, 35
Mountbatten, Lord Louis 31, 32
Mountbatten, Philip 33
Mussolini, Benito 24

Nagasaki 26
National Health Service 38
Nazis 8, 28, 29
Nehru, Pandit 32
New Look 31
Nkrumah, Kwame 41
Norway 8

Olympic Games 37
Orwell, George 41, 42

Palestine 28, 32, 33, 36, 37, 39
Paris 10, 21, 22, 30, 31, 33, 43
Pearl Harbor 13
Peking 39, 40
Philippines 13, 16, 23
Poland 8, 19, 21, 22
prefabs 23

Quisling, Vidkung 8

rationing 17, 30, 41
Red Army (Russian) 12, 15, 18, 22,
    23, 24
refugees 32, 39
Rommel, Erwin 13, 16
Roosevelt, Franklin D. 10, 14, 19,
    27
Royal Air Force 10, 17, 21
Royal Navy 8, 9, 12, 13
Russia (USSR) 8, 9, 15, 18, 19, 20,
    21, 22, 27, 28, 31, 33, 35, 36, 37,
    40

Singapore 16
Slim, William 26
South Africa 37, 40
Spaak, Paul Henri 28
Stalin, Joseph 10, 19
Stalingrad 15

Taiwan 40
Tobruk 13
Trotsky, Lev 10
Truman, Harry S. 27, 33, 37
United Kingdom 8, 9, 10, 11, 12,
    14, 17, 20, 23, 25, 27, 30, 31, 33,
    37, 38, 40, 41
United Nations Organization 27,
    29, 33, 36, 37
United States of America 10, 13,
    14, 17, 18, 22, 23, 24, 25, 27, 28,
    37, 39, 40

VE Day 25
Vietnam 29

Warsaw 19, 22